THE OFFICIAL
LIVERPOOL FC
ANNUAL
2016

W9-BNN-506

YOU'LL NEVER WALK ALONE

LIVERPOOL
FOOTBALL CLUB

EST·1892 ®

A Grange Publication

©2015. Published by Grange Communications Ltd., Edinburgh, under licence from The Liverpool Football Club and Athletic Grounds Ltd. Printed in the EU.

ISBN 978-1-910199-48-0

CONTENTS:

LIVERPOOL FOOTBALL CLUB

HONOURS BOARD

European Cup/UEFA Champions League Winners

1977, 1978, 1981, 1984, 2005

First Division Champions

1900/01, 1905/06, 1921/22, 1922/23, 1946/47, 1963/64, 1965/66, 1972/73, 1975/76, 1976/77, 1978/79, 1979/80, 1981/82, 1982/83, 1983/84, 1985/86, 1987/88, 1989/90

FA Cup Winners

1965, 1974, 1986, 1989, 1992, 2001, 2006

UEFA Cup Winners

1973, 1976, 2001

League Cup Winners

1981, 1982, 1983, 1984, 1995, 2001, 2003, 2012

Second Division Champions

1893/94, 1895/96, 1904/05, 1961/62

European Super Cup/ UEFA Super Cup Winners

1977, 2001, 2005

Screensport Super Cup Winners

1985/86

Charity/Community Shield Winners

1964*, 1965*, 1966, 1974, 1976, 1977*, 1979, 1980, 1982, 1986*, 1988, 1989, 1990*, 2001, 2006 (*shared)

FA Youth Cup Winners

1995/96, 2005/06, 2006/07

Reserve League Champions

1956/57, 1968/69, 1969/70, 1970/71, 1972/73, 1973/74, 1974/75, 1975/76, 1976/77, 1978/79, 1979/80, 1980/81, 1981/82, 1983/84, 1984/85, 1989/90, 1999/2000, 2007/08

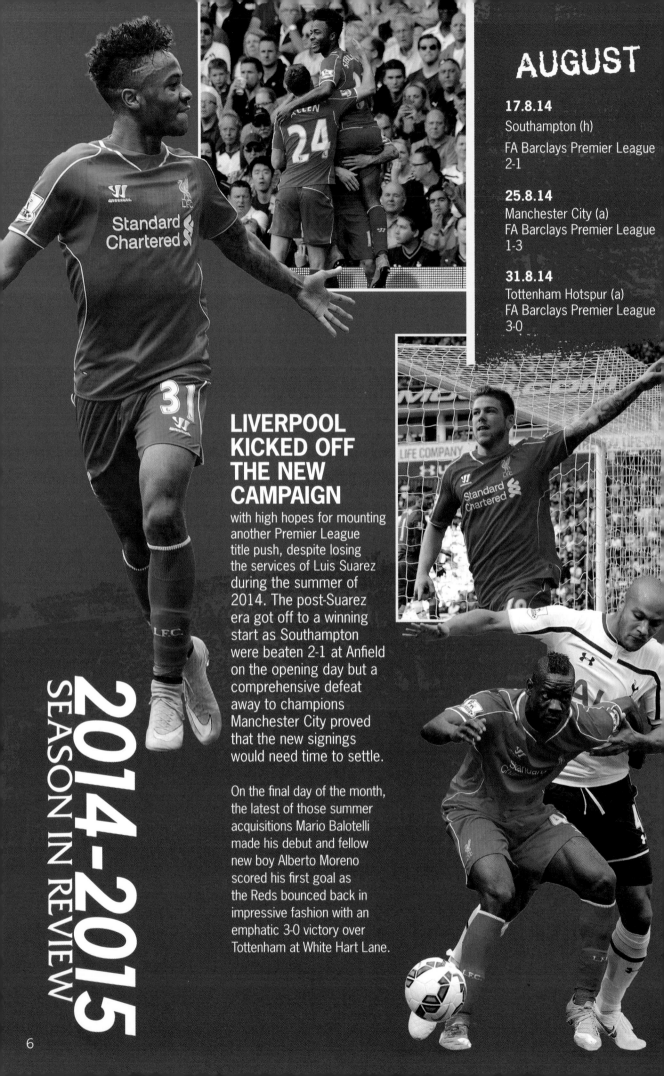

17.8.14
Southampton (h)
FA Barclays Premier League
2-1

25.8.14
Manchester City (a)
FA Barclays Premier League
1-3

31.8.14
Tottenham Hotspur (a)
FA Barclays Premier League
3-0

LIVERPOOL KICKED OFF THE NEW CAMPAIGN

with high hopes for mounting another Premier League title push, despite losing the services of Luis Suarez during the summer of 2014. The post-Suarez era got off to a winning start as Southampton were beaten 2-1 at Anfield on the opening day but a comprehensive defeat away to champions Manchester City proved that the new signings would need time to settle.

On the final day of the month, the latest of those summer acquisitions Mario Balotelli made his debut and fellow new boy Alberto Moreno scored his first goal as the Reds bounced back in impressive fashion with an emphatic 3-0 victory over Tottenham at White Hart Lane.

2014-2015 SEASON IN REVIEW

LIVERPOOL'S EARLY SEASON

inconsistency was clearly evident with just one point taken from nine in the FA Barclays Premier League during September.

It began when Aston Villa emerged surprise winners at Anfield and ended with a stunning last-gasp Phil Jagielka goal denying them all three points in the Merseyside derby. In between, Mario Balotelli got off the mark in a red shirt as Liverpool made their long awaited return to the Champions League, although it required a late Steven Gerrard penalty to spare their blushes and secure a narrow win over Bulgarian minnows Ludogorets on matchday one.

This month also saw the Reds get their Capital One Cup campaign underway but they made hard work of the 3rd round tie at home to Middlesbrough. Academy starlet Jordan Rossiter was handed his first senior start and marked the occasion by scoring the opener after just 10 minutes. However, the Championship side fought back and it needed a marathon penalty shoot-out before Liverpool's place in the next round was confirmed.

SEPTEMBER

13.9.14
Aston Villa (h)
FA Barclays Premier League
0-1

16.9.14
Ludogorets Razgrad (a)
Champions League Group B
2-1

20.9.14
West Ham United (a)
FA Barclays Premier League
1-3

23.9.14
Middlesbrough (h)
Capital One Cup 3rd round
2-2*

27.9.14
Everton (h)
FA Barclays Premier League
1-1

*Liverpool won 14-13 on penalties

7

DOMESTICALLY THIS WAS A DECENT MONTH FOR LIVERPOOL

but in Europe it was the complete opposite. They recorded back-to-back victories for the first time when defeating West Brom and QPR only to suffer successive losses in the Champions League. The visit to Anfield of reigning European champions Real Madrid was eagerly anticipated until the Spaniards quickly raced into a three-goal lead before half-time and threatened to run riot. Thankfully, the second half was not as one-sided and that's how the score remained. Coming on the back of a defeat in Basel, it left the Reds with a difficult task in terms of qualification from the group. In the Capital One Cup there were no such problems and further progress was made with a 2-1 win at home to Swansea City.

OCTOBER

1.10.14
Basel (a)
Champions League Group B
0-1

4.10.14
West Bromwich Albion (h)
FA Barclays Premier League
2-1

19.10.14
Queens Park Rangers (a)
FA Barclays Premier League
3-2

22.10.14
Real Madrid (h)
Champions League Group B
0-3

25.10.14
Hull City (h)
FA Barclays Premier League
0-0

28.10.14
Swansea City (h)
Capital One Cup 4th round
2-1

2014-2015 SEASON IN REVIEW

AS THE DARK NIGHTS CLOSED IN

Liverpool's season was in danger of imploding. Three straight Premier League defeats left the Reds languishing in mid-table, while their hopes of making it through to the knockout phase of the Champions League were hanging by a thread after taking just one point from a possible six. The only bright spot of a dismal month, apart from Rickie Lambert opening his Liverpool scoring account, was a home victory against Stoke, secured thanks to a solitary Glen Johnson goal five minutes from time.

NOVEMBER

1.11.14
Newcastle United (a)
FA Barclays Premier League
0-1

4.11.14
Real Madrid (a)
Champions League Group B
0-1

8.11.14
Chelsea (h)
FA Barclays Premier League
1-2

23.11.14
Crystal Palace (a)
FA Barclays Premier League
1-3

26.11.14
Ludogorets Razgrad (a)
Champions League Group B
2-2

29.11.14
Stoke City (h)
FA Barclays Premier League
1-0

LIVERPOOL ULTIMATELY ENDED 2014 ON A HIGH

but first had to endure the disappointments of bowing out of the Champions League at the group stage and then suffering a heavy defeat away to rivals Machester United.

A place in the last four of the Capital One Cup was secured at the expense of high-flying Championship outfit Bournemouth, when many pundits were predicting an upset, and the Reds then went on to provide plenty of festive cheer for their supporters. A last-minute Martin Skrtel goal rescued a point at home to Arsenal before Burnley and Swansea were defeated in the final two games of the calendar year.

2014-2015 SEASON IN REVIEW

DECEMBER

2.12.14
Leicester City (a)
FA Barclays Premier League
3-1

6.12.14
Sunderland (h)
FA Barclays Premier League
0-0

9.12.14
Basel (h)
Champions League Group B
1-1

14.12.14
Manchester United (a)
FA Barclays Premier League
0-3

17.12.14
Bournemouth (a)
Capital One Cup 5th round
3-1

21.12.14
Arsenal (h)
FA Barclays Premier League
2-2

26.12.14
Burnley (a)
FA Barclays Premier League
1-0

29.12.14
Swansea City (h)
FA Barclays Premier League
4-1

JANUARY

1.1.15
Leicester City (h)
FA Barclays Premier League
2-2

5.1.15
AFC Wimbledon (a)
FA Cup 3rd round
2-1

10.1.15
Sunderland (a)
FA Barclays Premier League
1-0

17.1.15
Aston Villa (a)
FA Barclays Premier League
2-0

20.1.15
Chelsea (h)
Capital One Cup semi-final 1st leg
1-1

24.1.15
Bolton Wanderers (h)
FA Cup 4th round
0-0

27.1.15
Chelsea (h)
Capital One Cup semi-final 2nd leg
0-1

31.1.14
West Ham United (h)
FA Barclays Premier League
2-0

THE NEW YEAR SAW ONE DOOR TO WEMBLEY OPEN

for Liverpool and another close. A narrow two-legged defeat to eventual winners Chelsea in the Capital One Cup semi-final was a bitter pill to swallow but the FA Cup trail began with Steven Gerrard, fresh from announcing that he was to be leaving Anfield at the end of the season, scoring twice as a potential banana-skin was avoided away to League Two's AFC Wimbledon in round three. On the Premier League front Liverpool picked up where they had left off in December and stretched their unbeaten run to seven games, the highlights being successive victories on the road against Sunderland and Aston Villa.

LIVERPOOL'S IMPROVED RUN

of form was carried over into February, with the two most significant triumphs coming against fellow top four challengers Tottenham, courtesy of a Mario Balotelli winner, and Southampton, where Philippe Coutinho opened the scoring with a stunning goal of the season contender. The little Brazilian was playing out of his skin and earlier in the month it was another of his goals that secured a dramatic fourth round replay at Bolton. Away to Crystal Palace in the next round Daniel Sturridge and Adam Lallana were on the scoresheet, as Liverpool came from behind to clinch a place in the quarter-final. The only downside to the month came in the Europa League where a penalty shoot-out defeat to Besiktas ended Liverpool's interest in the competition.

FEBRUARY

4.2.15
Bolton Wanderers (a)
FA Cup 4th round replay
2-1

7.2.15
Everton (a)
FA Barclays Premier League
0-0

10.2.15
Tottenham Hotspur (h)
FA Barclays Premier League
3-2

14.2.15
Crystal Palace (a)
FA Cup 5th round
2-1

19.2.15
Besiktas (h)
Europa League round of 32
1st leg
1-0

22.2.15
Southampton (a)
FA Barclays Premier League
2-0

26.2.15
Besiktas (a)
Europea League round of 32
2nd leg
0-1*

*(*Liverpool lost 4-5 on penalties)*

2014-2015 SEASON IN REVIEW

A MONTH THAT WAS BOOK-ENDED

by contrasting results at home to the two Manchester clubs. It started in a blaze of glory with champions Manchester City being vanquished in front of the Kop for the second season running and, again, it was man-of-the-moment Coutinho who took the plaudits with another spectacular match-winning strike. League doubles were then completed over Burnley and Swansea before Manchester United burst the bubble by running out 2-1 winners at Anfield, a game in which Steven Gerrard was given his marching orders just 40 seconds after coming on as a half-time substitute.

MARCH

1.3.15
Manchester City (h)
FA Barclays Premier League
2-1

4.3.15
Burnley (h)
FA Barclays Premier League
2-0

8.3.15
Blackburn Rovers (h)
FA Cup 5th round
0-0

16.3.15
Swansea City (a)
FA Barclays
Premier League
1-0

22.3.15
Manchester
United (h)
FA Barclays
Premier League
1-2

IN THE SPACE OF LESS THAN A FORTNIGHT

Liverpool's FA Cup dream soared then sunk. A goal from who else but Coutinho settled a hard-fought quarter-final replay victory against Blackburn at Ewood Park but despite starting as favourites in the semi-final at Wembley, Aston Villa put paid to any plans of a return to the capital for the final in May. In front of 85,000 at the national stadium goals from Christian Benteke and Fabian Delph cancelled out an earlier Coutinho strike meaning Liverpool's season was now in danger of petering out – a fact confirmed when they ended the month with a disappointing goalless draw at the Hawthorns, then a shock 1-0 defeat to relegation-threatened Hull.

2014-2015 SEASON IN REVIEW

14

APRIL

4.4.15
Asenal (a)
FA Barclays Premier League
1-4

8.4.15
Blackburn Rovers (a)
FA Cup 5th round replay
1-0

13.4.15
Newcastle United (h)
FA Barclays Premier League
2-0

19.4.15
Aston Villa (a)
FA Cup semi-final
1-2

25.4.15
West Bromwich Albion (a)
FA Barclays Premier League
0-0

28.4.15
Hull City (a)
FA Barclays Premier League
0-1

THE FINAL MONTH OF THE SEASON WAS ALL ABOUT ONE MAN.

As the curtain came down on Steven Gerrard's illustrious Liverpool career, the captain was determined to savour every remaining minute in a red shirt and he rolled back the years to head home a late winner at the Kop end against QPR then threatened to spoil the celebrations at Stamford Bridge by scoring the opener against the recently crowned champions. His final appearance at Anfield was an emotional one. Not even a 3-1 defeat to Crystal Palace could ruin the occasion and many a tear was shed when he embarked on a lap of honour at the end. The season ended at the Britannia Stadium and the least said about that the better. On an afternoon to forget, Stoke inflicted Liverpool's heaviest defeat for over 50 years, the only bright spot being that the departing skipper signed off with a goal.

MAY

2.5.15
Queens Park Rangers (h)
FA Barclays Premier League
2-1

10.5.15
Chelsea (a)
FA Barclays Premier League
1-1

16.5.15
Crystal Palace (h)
FA Barclays Premier League
1-3

24.5.15
Stoke City (a)
FA Barclays Premier League
1-6

WELCOME

During what was a busy summer of transfer activity, no less than seven new faces arrived at the gates of Melwood during the 2015 close season. Here's what they had to say upon putting pen to paper with the Reds...

ROBERTO FIRMINO
(from 1899 Hoffenheim)

"As a football fan, I've been watching the Premier League for a while now. Liverpool was my choice because of its history and its team, and also because Coutinho told me some great things about the club. I hope I can bring joy to the people playing for this club."

"Liverpool is a great fit for me as a club. It's a huge club and there is a lot of pressure every time you step out onto that field. I've played in front of the Anfield crowd and it'll be nice to be on the other side of the fans now! The atmosphere they create is fantastic and probably some of the best atmospheres I've played in, in England, so to have them supporting me is definitely going to be an amazing feeling."

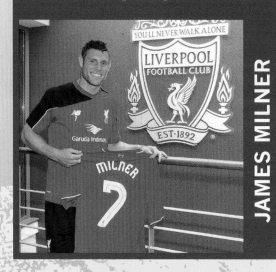

JAMES MILNER
(from Manchester City)

CHRISTIAN BENTEKE
(from Aston Villa)

"I'm very happy to be part of the Liverpool family now and I will do everything to make them happy and work hard for them and my teammates. When I came here with Aston Villa it was a great feeling to play at Anfield. I know Liverpool is a big story. They've won [many] league titles and the Champions League five times and of course the UEFA Cup and a lot of trophies. I know it's a big club. I came here to win trophies. I came here to reach some great goals with the team."

"Words can't describe the move that I've got for myself. But, at the same time, I've worked my way up from the bottom so it's even more special for me. It's a challenge I'm looking forward to, I'd never get complacent with anything like that. Now I've got that move, I'll work even harder to try and get into that team and be the best professional I can be."

DANNY INGS
(from Burnley)

TO LIVERPOOL

NATHANIEL CLYNE
(from Southampton)

"I'm here for the long-term. I'm looking to nail a spot down at Liverpool as soon as possible, but I still have a number of things I can improve on that will hopefully make me a better player than I am now. I'm confident that I can help the team and that we can have a good season. I've seen lots of great atmospheres at Anfield, especially on the European nights, so it will be exciting to experience that. Seeing the crowd hold up their scarves and sing 'You'll Never Walk Alone' from the perspective of a Liverpool player will be good."

"It's important to be at a good club where people believe in you and where you feel good. I had a very good feeling about Liverpool. It's a good club and they have experience of working with young players. The most important thing is that I work hard and then I think everything will be OK. Liverpool is a wonderful club that deserves to be at the top. It will be on us, the players, to give everything."

DIVOCK ORIGI
(from Lille)

JOE GOMEZ
(from Charlton Athletic)

"It was flattering to know that a massive club like this were interested in me. That was one of the main things - I knew how great the club is. That's why it was an easy decision to come here. To know that a place like this was interested and knew about me was great. It's a dream come true."

"Liverpool is one of the most famous clubs in the world. When I was young, watching football and wanting to be a football player, I was watching a lot of games. I remember the [2001] UEFA Cup final and also the [2005] Champions League final. Everybody in Hungary knows about Liverpool and everybody knows what a big club it is, so I knew a lot."

ADAM BOGDAN
(from Bolton Wanderers)

A BRIEF HISTORY OF THE LIVERPOOL KIT

1955

1969

1892 The first-ever Liverpool team run out sporting blue and white halved shirts.

1896 The most significant change in the history of Liverpool's kit sees the club adopt red shirts and white shorts as their home colours.

1950 A badge is worn on the Liverpool shirt for the first time. The occasion was the club's second FA Cup Final appearance and their first at Wembley.

1955 Midway through the 1955/56 season the Liver Bird takes pride of place on the home shirt for the first time.

1964 The now famous all-red home kit is born. Bill Shankly gets his captain Ron Yeats to act as the model and instantly declares that it makes him look 'seven foot tall'.

1969 The crest on the shirt is redesigned and the stand alone Liver Bird motif, that adorns the shirt today, is introduced.

1973	A manufacturer's logo is displayed on the shirt for the first time.
1979	Liverpool become the first club in the Football League to wear shirts emblazoned with the name of a sponsor.
1982	A revolutionary pin-stripe design is unveiled for the home and away shirt.
1987	The official club crest which had been used for administration and merchandising purposes since the early seventies appears on the kit for the first time.

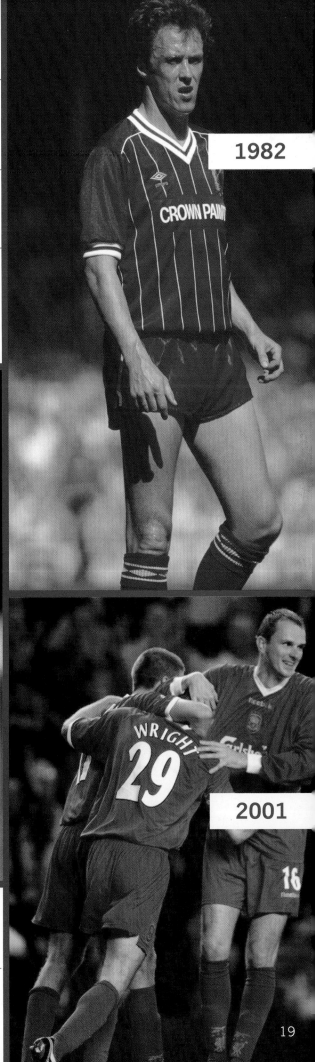

1982

1992

2001

1992	To commemorate the club's centenary the crest on the shirt is changed again.
2001	An alternative home strip is used in European games for the first time.

19

2012

The stand alone Liver Bird makes a welcome return to the shirt, while the victims of the Hillsborough disaster are honoured on the back with two eternal flames alongside the number 96

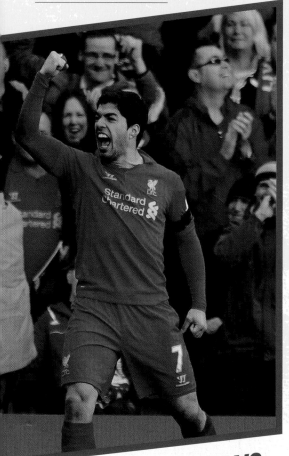

SHIRT SPONSORS

1979-82: Hitachi
1982-88: Crown Paints
1988-92: Candy
1992-2010: Carlsberg
2010–present: Standard Chartered

KIT MANUFACTURERS

1973-85: Umbro
1985-96: Adidas
1996-2006: Reebok
2006-12: Adidas
2012-15: Warrior
2015: New Balance

AWAY KIT COLOURS

1892-1982: White
1982-85: Yellow
1985-87: White
1987-91: Silver/Grey
1991-93: Green
1993-95: Green/White
1995-96: Green/White quarters
1996-97: Ecru
1997-98: Yellow
1998-99: White
1999-2000: Green/Navy
2000-01: Gold/Navy
2001-02: White/Navy
2002-03: Black/Grey
2004-04: White
2004-05: Yellow
2005-06: White
2006-07: Yellow
2007-08: White
2008-09: Silver/Grey
2009-10: Black
2010-11: White
2011-12: Dark Grey
2012-13: Black
2013-14: White
2014-15: Yellow
2015-16: White

3RD KIT COLOURS

1979-82: Yellow
1988-87: Yellow
1988-89: White
1994-96: Gold/Black
1998-99: Yellow
1999-2000: White
2000-01: Green/Navy
2001-02: Gold/Navy
2002-03: White/Navy
2004-04: Black/Grey
2004-05: White
2005-06: Yellow
2006-07: White/Green
2007-08: Black
2008-09: Green
2009-10: White
2010-11: Black
2011-12: White
2012-13: Purple
2013-14: Purple/White/Black
2014-15: Black
2015-16: Black

DID YOU KNOW?

On a number of occasions between 1911 and 1920 Liverpool are known to have worn striped shirts as an alternative to their normal away strip

Liverpool wore blue and white hooped socks in the 1950 FA Cup final

Before switching to all-red in 1964, the socks Liverpool wore with their red shirts and white shorts fluctuated between black, red, white and red/white hoops

At home to Ajax in 1966, Liverpool wore a one-off 3rd strip of canary yellow shirts, black shorts and yellow socks

The last time Liverpool wore their away colours at home was in 1998 against Valencia in the UEFA Cup

Liverpool have twice produced alternative home kits for use in European competition only (2001-03 and 2005-06)

The first time players' names were displayed on the back of a Liverpool shirt was in December 1981 for the World Club Championship clash with Flamengo in Tokyo

Away to Watford in 1984 Liverpool wore an unusual combination of red shirts, black shorts and yellow socks

To avoid a clash with the red socks worn by Portsmouth, Liverpool have sported both black and white socks with their usual red home strip during games at Fratton Park

DESIGN YOUR OWN KIT

HAVE A GO at showing your artistic talent by designing your own Liverpool FC kit!

Colours?
(red, maybe?)

Any new patterns or details this year?

Where does the badge go?

Shall we change the socks this year?

Boots?

How about a ball?

GOALS OF THE SEASON

A countdown of the top ten goals scored by Liverpool during the 2014/15 campaign…

10. Jordan Henderson v Burnley
(h) FA Barclays Premier League: 4 March 2015

After Coutinho's initial shot was blocked, the in-rushing Henderson was ideally placed and as the ball rebounded to him on the edge of the box he made no mistake, arrowing a first time pile-driver through the crowded penalty area and into the net.

9. Raheem Sterling v Chelsea
(h) Capital One Cup semi-final 1st leg: 20 January 2015

Dropping deep to receive the ball, Sterling expertly turned Nemanja Matic and advanced towards goal from a central position. Using his pace to full effect he made space and once inside the area unleashed a low shot past Courtois to draw Liverpool level.

8. Steven Gerrard v Everton
(h) FA Barclays Premier League: 27 September 2014

This was to be Gerrard's last goal against the old enemy and he made sure it was one to remember by breaking the deadlock with a free-kick which he accurately lifted over the wall and beyond the despairing dive of Blues 'keeper Tim Howard.

7. Adam Lallana v West Bromwich Albion
(h) FA Barclays Premier League: 4 October 2014

It took Lallana seven games to break his scoring duck for the Reds but when it came it was worth the wait; some silky skills on the edge of the box being followed by a defence-splitting one-two with Jordan Henderson and a clinical left-footed finish.

6. Alberto Moreno v Tottenham Hotspur
(a) FA Barclays Premier League: 31 August 2014

In just his second game for the club Moreno got off the mark in impressive fashion, dispossessing Andros Townsend deep inside the Liverpool half and charging up field before cutting inside from the left and drilling a low shot into bottom far corner.

5. Jordan Henderson v Manchester City
(h) FA Barclays Premier League: 1 March 2015

In a move reminiscent of the high-tempo style of the previous season, the Reds broke swiftly. Coutinho intercepted a pass on the halfway line and fed Sterling who raced forward. The ball was squared to Henderson and he then took a step to the right and, from the edge of the area, curled a sublime shot into the far top corner.

4. Steven Gerrard v Basel
(h) Champions League Group Phase B: December 2014

A second free-kick entrant from the captain, this strike ultimately wasn't enough to keep Liverpool in the Champions League but it was the highlight of an otherwise disappointing night; a right-footed effort from 30-yards out that curled over the wall and nestled sweetly into the top corner.

3. Philippe Coutinho v Bolton Wanderers
(a) FA Cup 4th round replay: 4 February 2015

With extra-time looming Coutinho fashioned a moment of magic to seal Liverpool's passage into round five. Accepting a pass to the left of the goal, he took just two touches before letting fly with a stunning drive that looped into the far top corner.

2. Philippe Coutinho v Manchester City
(h) FA Barclays Premier League: 1 March 2015

There didn't appear to be much danger when Coutinho initially took possession but he proceeded to settle a tense battle against the reigning champions by skillfully sidestepping Samir Nasri and beating Joe Hart with an unstoppable curling drive into the top corner of the Kop net.

1. Philippe Coutinho v Southampton
(a) FA Barclays Premier League: 22 February 2015

Just 2 minutes and 43 seconds had elapsed when Coutinho produced the undoubted moment of this match. The little Brazilian started and finished the move; making space by playing a clever one-two with Markovic then, with a little back-lift, hammering home a 30-yard shot that went in off the underside of the bar.

ANFIELD ALL-STARS

Some of the biggest names in Liverpool's recent history

rolled back the years to grace the hallowed Anfield turf one more time – all in the name of charity.

The likes of Luis Suarez, Xabi Alonso, Fernando Torres, Pepe Reina and Luis Garcia were given a fantastic reception when they returned for the All-Star Charity game in March 2015.

The match was organized by Liverpool FC Foundation and a capacity crowd ensured it was a tremendous success.

A Steven Gerrard XI took on a Jamie Carragher XI, with both teams containing a mix of current and former Liverpool players, plus some specially invited guests that included Thierry Henry, John Terry and Didier Drogba. Fittingly, the end result was a 2-2 draw, with goals from Mario Balotelli and Drogba firing Carra's side into a two-goal lead before Gerrard drew his team level with a brace of penalties.

The supporters were in fine voice throughout as they worked through their repertoire of songs to honour the former Kop favourites

and one of the undoubted highlights of the afternoon came just after half-time when Suarez and Torres linked up to spearhead a mouth-watering attack.

At the final whistle both squads showed their appreciation by embarking on a joint lap of honour and everyone was in agreement that it had been a truly memorable occasion, with £1 million raised for Liverpool FC Foundation and its local partner charities.

gerrard XI

Jones (Vigouroux)
Johnson
A Gerrard (Dann)
Terry (Williams)
Riise (Warnock)
S Gerrard (Teixeira)
Alonso (Teixeira, Spearing)
Nolan (Adam)
Babel
Sinclair (Torres)
Henry (Suarez).

carragher XI

Reina (Gulacsi)
Flanagan (Moreno)
Kelly
Carragher
Arbeloa (Clichy)
Lucas (Maguire)
Shelvey (Noone)
Downing (Borini)
Kewell (Bellamy)
Drogba (Garcia)
Balotelli (Brannagan)

THE BIG KOP QUIZ

1. From which club did Liverpool sign Roberto Firmino?

2. At which ground did Liverpool first win the League Cup?

3. Who was the only Liverpool player to feature in the 2014/15 PFA Team of the Year?

4. What club did Bill Shankly manage immediately before joining Liverpool?

5. In which city did Liverpool kick-off their 2015 summer tour?

6. Who did Liverpool beat to win their first European trophy in 1973?

7. Which Liverpool player was on the losing side in the final of the 2015 UEFA European under-21 Championships?

8. Who scored on his Liverpool debut at home to Middlesbrough in last season's Capital One Cup?

9. Against which club did Steven Gerrard score his first Liverpool hat-trick?

10. For which country did Divock Origi star at the 2014 World Cup in Brazil?

11. What colour shirts did Liverpool wear in the 1977 FA Cup final?

12. Which current Liverpool striker played against the Reds in the final of the 2006 FA Youth Cup?

13. In terms of medals won, who is the most decorated Liverpool player of all-time?

14. Which former Liverpool player scored in the 2015 Champions League final?

15. How many games did Anfield host at Euro 96?

(answers on p.61)

16. Which Liverpool Ladies player scored England's goal in the 2015 FIFA Women's World Cup semi-final?

TRUE OR FALSE?

17. Kenny Dalglish once scored at
    Anfield for a team other than Liverpool _____

18. Ian Rush was on the books for
    Everton as a youngster _____

19. Dirk Kuyt scored the winning goal for
    Liverpool in the 2012 Carling Cup final _____

20. Nathaniel Clyne has a tattoo of himself
    as a three-year old on his arm _____

WHO AM I ?

21. I supported Liverpool as a boy but played for Everton; in the summer of 2000 I crossed
    Stanley Park to sign for the Reds and scored on my derby debut. _____

22. I joined Liverpool from Scunthorpe United in 1971, scored twice in the 1974 FA Cup final
    and later left to play in West Germany. _____

23. I was born in Israel, scored hat-tricks for Liverpool in the Premier League, FA Cup and
    Champions League, and played for both Chelsea and Arsenal after leaving Anfield.
    _____

NAME THE YEAR

24. Liverpool wore all-red for the first time, won the
    First Division Championship and played KR Reykjavik
    in the European Cup. _____

25. Kenny Dalglish made his Liverpool debut,
    David Fairclough scored his famous goal against
    St Etienne and the League title was secured with a
    goalless draw at home to West Ham. _____

26. The Anfield Rap reached number three in the UK
    music charts, John Barnes won Player of the Year and
    Ian Rush returned from Juventus. _____

27. Liverpool reached the Champions League final in
    Athens, Fernando Torres joined the club from
    Atletico Madrid and Besiktas were beaten 8-0 at Anfield. _____

FILL IN THE MISSING GAPS

28. Before joining Liverpool, James Milner played for Leeds, Newcastle, _____ and
    Manchester City

29. Liverpool won the UEFA Cup in 1973, _____ and 2001

30. In the 2005 Champions League final, Liverpool's goalscorers in the penalty shoot-out
    were Djibril Cisse, _____ and Vladimir Smicer

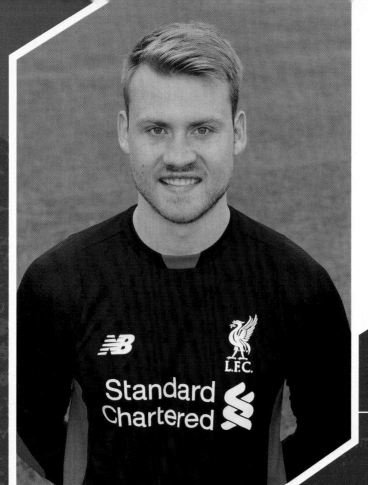

SIMON MIGNOLET

DATE OF BIRTH:
6 March 1988

BIRTHPLACE:
Sint-Truiden, Belgium

PREVIOUS CLUBS:
Sint-Truiden, Sunderland

SIGNED:
June 2013

PLAYER

DATE OF BIRTH:
27 September 1987

BIRTHPLACE:
Birthplace: Budapest, Hungary

PREVIOUS CLUBS:
Previous clubs: Vasas,
Vecses (loan),
Bolton Wanderers,
Crewe Alexandra (loan)

SIGNED:
July 2015

ADAM BOGDAN

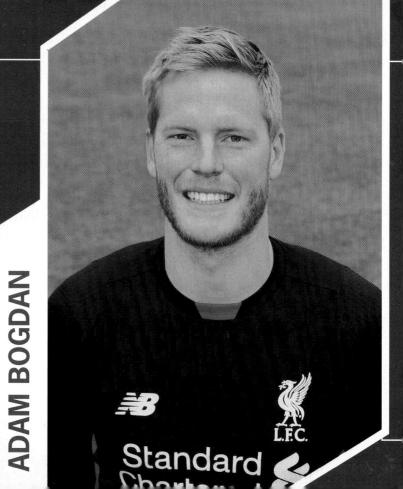

NATHANIEL CLYNE

DATE OF BIRTH:
5 April 1991

BIRTHPLACE:
Stockwell

PREVIOUS CLUBS:
Crystal Palace, Southampton

SIGNED:
July 2015

PROFILES

DATE OF BIRTH:
1 January 1993

BIRTHPLACE:
Liverpool

PREVIOUS CLUBS:
none

SIGNED:
2007 (Academy)

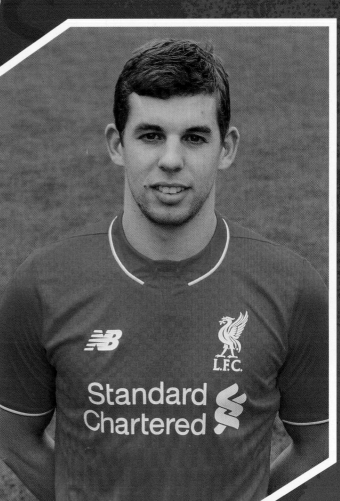

JON FLANAGAN

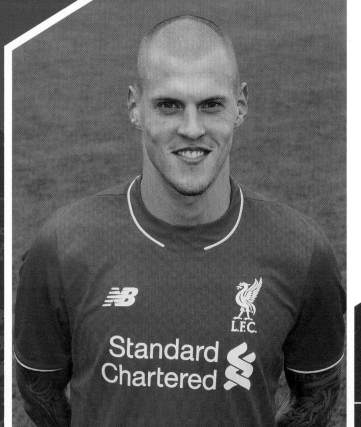

MARTIN SKRTEL

DATE OF BIRTH:
15 December 1984

BIRTHPLACE:
Handlova, Slovakia

PREVIOUS CLUBS:
Trencin, Zenit St Petersburg

SIGNED:
January 2008

PLAYER

DATE OF BIRTH:
5 July 1989

BIRTHPLACE:
Zenica, Bosnia & Herzegovina

PREVIOUS CLUBS:
Dinamo Zagreb,
Inter Zapresic (loan),
Lyon, Southampton

SIGNED:
July 2014

DEJAN LOVREN

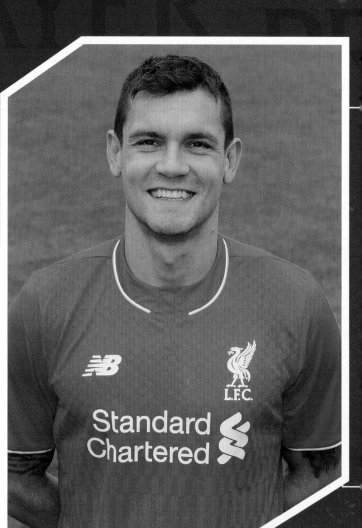

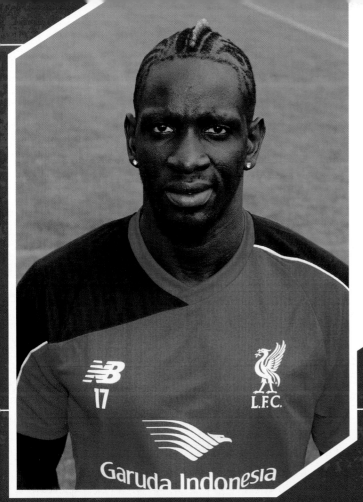

MAMADOU SAKHO

DATE OF BIRTH:
13 February 1990

BIRTHPLACE:
Paris, France

PREVIOUS CLUBS:
Paris St Germain

SIGNED:
September 2013

PROFILES

DATE OF BIRTH:
19 March 1981

BIRTHPLACE:
Bouake, Ivory Coast

PREVIOUS CLUBS:
ASEC Mimosas,
Arsenal, Manchester City

SIGNED:
July 2013

KOLO TOURE

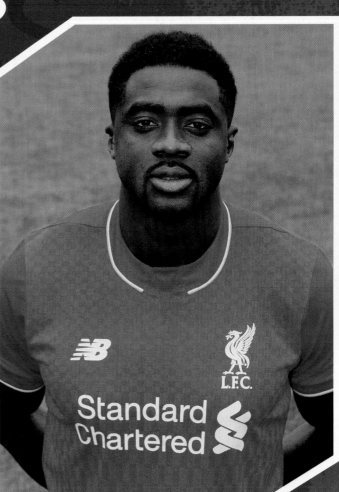

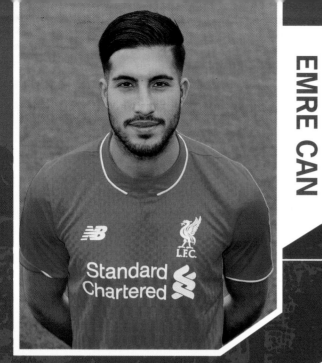

EMRE CAN

DATE OF BIRTH:
12 January 1984

BIRTHPLACE:
Frankfurt, Germany

PREVIOUS CLUBS:
Bayern Munich, Bayer Leverkusen

SIGNED:
June 2014

DATE OF BIRTH:
5 July 1992

BIRTHPLACE:
Seville, Spain

PREVIOUS CLUBS:
Sevilla

SIGNED:
August 2014

ALBERTO MORENO

PLAYER PROFILES

JOE GOMEZ

DATE OF BIRTH:
12 January 1984

BIRTHPLACE:
Catford

PREVIOUS CLUBS:
Charlton Athletic

SIGNED:
June 2015

LUCAS LEIVA

DATE OF BIRTH:
9 January 1987

BIRTHPLACE:
Dourados, Brazil

PREVIOUS CLUBS:
Gremio

SIGNED:
May 2007

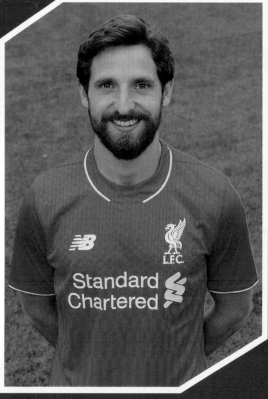

JOE ALLEN

DATE OF BIRTH:
14 March 1990

BIRTHPLACE:
Carmarthen, Wales

PREVIOUS CLUBS:
Swansea City

SIGNED:
August 2012

PLAYER
PROFILES

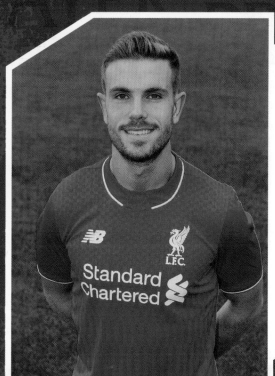

JORDAN HENDERSON

DATE OF BIRTH:
17 June 1990

BIRTHPLACE:
Sunderland

PREVIOUS CLUBS:
Sunderland, Coventry City (loan)

SIGNED:
June 2011

33

COUTINHO-OH-OH!

Liverpool's little magician Phil Coutinho is one of the most popular players among the fans at Anfield. He was the club's undoubted star man during the 2014/15 season and looks to have a glittering future ahead of him.

This is him in his own words...

GROWING UP IN RIO...

"I was like any other child. I played a lot, and was quite troublesome for my parents. I also enjoyed time with my brothers. I wanted to do things they were doing. We had enough food at home, my father always worked."

HIS TIME AT INTER MILAN...

"It was the hardest point of my career because it was the first time I had been away from home and I had to start proving myself from scratch."

PLAYING FUTSAL...

"I love futsal! In Brazil, many boys stop playing futsal and move to 11-a-side, as it is too much to be playing both. I did not want to leave futsal at all, so I played until I was thirteen, fourteen, and then I had to stop it. I've always liked futsal. It's really fun. The small ball, restricted space, I really enjoyed it."

LIVING IN LIVERPOOL...

"I'm really happy here. At the club, in the city. The city is really calm. The people here are really sympathetic, they are very cheerful. It all helps. On the field we try to be happy, cheerful, for the things to go as planned."

ADAPTING TO ENGLISH FOOTBALL...

"Where I come from we play football differently, it's more intense here. Here we have to defend more, use the body. I believe I have learned and improved on this, but I think that I must always improve. There are many things to improve, so I'll never be in my comfort zone."

BEING A LIVERPOOL PLAYER...

"The club is like a family here, everybody is treated equally, from the youngest to the most senior players, and the club has the perfect structure for us to work. The club believed in me and I'm very thankful to them."

LOVING THE GAME...

"It's so much more than work. Football is what I like to do. I love to play football. I've always loved it, when I was young it was all about football. Football is my passion. Whenever I play, I think of my wife, my father, my mother, my brothers, they are the people who always support me."

HIS 'O MAGICO' BANNER ON THE KOP...

"I was really honoured. I remember we went to the field for warming up, and the banner was there, and it gave me goose bumps. I got really excited, I found it really cool. It's very good to receive this warmth from the fans and I want to thank them for the effort."

WHEN LIVERPOOL FANS SING HIS NAME...

"It is a unique and special feeling. It's incredible when I hear the song, and it is touching that there are people who connect with you."

THE FUTURE...

"I have many. I want to be part of the Brazilian national team, to be playing, to be a great player and win titles. This is the most important thing. It's what makes you become an idol in the club. This is what marks the club. I have this ambition, this goal of participating and winning titles."

A CAPTAIN'S FAREWELL

It was with a heavy heart that Liverpool supporters said farewell to Steven Gerrard in May 2015. As one of the club's greatest-ever players he will be sorely missed by everyone at Anfield.

A boyhood Liverpudlian who had been with the club since the age of eight, Gerrard lived the ultimate dream during an illustrious career with the Reds.

It may seem strange to now see him in a different shirt but as he embarks on a new life with LA Galaxy let's be thankful of the memories he leaves behind.

Goal-line clearance v Everton

On his derby debut, an 18-year old Gerrard came off the bench and made a vital defensive contribution as Liverpool hung on to record their first win over Everton for five years.

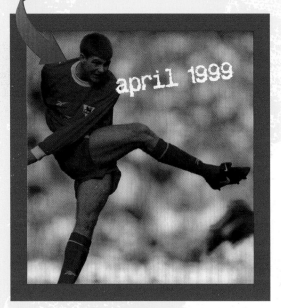
april 1999

march 2004

Bursting the back of the United net

With his stature as one of the country's most promising young players growing by the week Gerrard hit a 30-yard screamer that flew past Fabien Barthez and set Liverpool on their way to a 2-0 victory against Manchester United.

Olympiacos goal

The Reds were heading out of the Champions League at the group phase until Gerrard's heroic 86th minute intervention kept them on the road to Istanbul and forced Andy Gray to scream 'you beauty!'

december 2004

may 2005

Lifting the Champions League

The undoubted highlight of Gerrard's time at the club came at the Ataturk Stadium in Istanbul when he captained Liverpool to the greatest comeback in football history as a 3-0 half-time deficit was overturned against AC Milan.

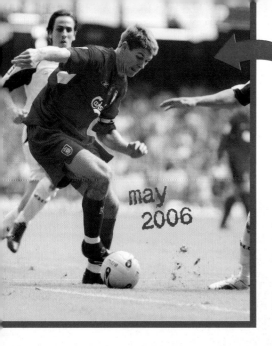

may 2006

The 'Gerrard final'

No player has stamped his authority on an FA Cup final like Gerrard did against West Ham at the Millennium Stadium, Cardiff. In what was a truly inspirational performance, the skipper struck two memorable goals to rescue the Reds from the brink of defeat.

march 2009

A brace to beat Madrid

Gerrard helped ensure that Real Madrid's first ever visit to Anfield was one they'd rather forget. He scored a goal in each half as Liverpool completed an emphatic 5-0 aggregate victory in the last 16 of the Champions League.

february 2012

Leading Liverpool up the steps at Wembley

Following a dramatic penalty shoot-out triumph over Cardiff in the final of the Carling Cup, Gerrard became the first Liverpool captain to lift a trophy at the new Wembley.

march 2012

Hat-trick hero v Everton

Not since Ian Rush in 1982 had a player scored three goals in a Merseyside derby but this Gerrard treble sunk the Blues without trace on another unforgettable night at Anfield.

A YEAR IN THE LIFE
OF MIGHTY RED

'It's been another busy 12 months for Liverpool's official mascot Mighty Red, here are some snaps from his album...'

A selfie with my good friend Sir SIB, the Standard Chartered masco

Having some fun in Bangkok at our Pre-season game

Lending my support to the LFC Ladies at the Halton Stadium

Getting ready for action at the Merseyside school games

At the Academy to practice my football skills at the club's Easter Soccer School

Showing racism the red card with LFC ambassador Robbie Fowler

Making flags with my friends at All Saints Catholic Primary school

Posing with Mamadou Sakho and Alberto Moreno in Australia

Spreading some cheer around the wards at the Alder Hey Children's Hospital

Pre-match fun with some friends in Australia

My bag is packed and I'm all set to jet off on the pre-season tour

Meeting one of my heroes — LFC legend Luis Garcia

CAPTAIN FANTASTIC

In accepting the role of Liverpool's new full-time captain, Jordan Henderson is following in the footsteps of some of the club's all-time greats...

Andrew Hannah
1892-1895

Having previously captained Everton during their days at Anfield, he became Liverpool's first-ever captain and was a key figure during the club's formative years.

Alex Raisbeck
1900-1909

The club's first title-winning captain and a commanding presence around Anfield, he skippered Liverpool to glory in 1901 and repeated the feat five years later.

Matt Busby
1939-1940

His reign as captain was prematurely cut short by the war but he made such an impression while wearing the armband that when supporters voted for an all-time LFC XI in 1966 they were unanimous that he should be skipper.

Phil Taylor
1950-1953

Holds the distinction of being the first captain to lead a Liverpool team out at Wembley, when Liverpool played Arsenal in the 1950 FA Cup final.

Billy Liddell
1955-1958

Captained Liverpool with great dignity during the dark days of life in the Second Division; leading by example on and off the pitch.

Ron Yeats
1961-1970

Led Liverpool out of the Second Division and into Europe, lifting two league titles and a first-ever FA Cup for the club in the process.

Tommy Smith
1970-1973

The first Liverpool captain to be presented with a European trophy, he was the proud recipient of the UEFA Cup in 1973, the year in which he also guided the Reds to the Championship.

Emlyn Hughes
1973-1979

A double European Cup winning captain, Crazy Horse's beaming smile lit up the continent in 1977 and 1978, while his infectious enthusiasm rubbed off on all those around him.

Phil Thompson
1979-1982

This former Kopite fulfilled a boyhood dream when lifting the European Cup in Paris in May 1981. He also led Liverpool to success in the First Division and League Cup.

Graeme Souness
1982-1984

The inspirational figure behind the treble triumph of 1983/84 and arguably the toughest skipper in Liverpool's history, he suffered fools gladly and was always at the forefront of the battle.

Alan Hansen
1985-1988 & 1989-90

Renowned for his ice-cool composure, he capped his first season in possession of the armband by captaining the Reds to an historic League and FA Cup double in 1985/86.

Sami Hyypia
2000-2003

Quiet and dignified but hugely respected, the big Finn was stand-in skipper during the triple trophy winning season of 2000/01 before accepting the role on a permanent basis in 2002.

Steven Gerrard
2003-2015

The longest-serving captain in Liverpool history, his herculean efforts regularly rescued the team; most notably in Istanbul (2005) and Cardiff (2006) when the Champions League and FA Cup were won.

JORDAN HENDERSON ON BECOMING CAPTAIN

"I'm absolutely delighted and proud. It is a great honour and a huge privilege to be named as the captain of this football club. When Steven [Gerrard] wasn't in the team last season, I tried to do the best I could when I stepped in and took the armband. Now I'll be looking to carry that on and continue to grow as a captain. I'll look to give my best all of the time, put the team firmly first and try to give them - or help them with - whatever they need from me."

BRENDAN RODGERS ON HANDING THE CAPTAINCY TO JORDAN HENDERSON:

"Jordan is someone who leads through example - through his actions, attitude and application. He shows total commitment to the game and is a role model professional. He is also greatly respectful of the great traditions associated with being Liverpool captain and the responsibilities that come with it. He has been blessed to learn first-hand from one of the greatest the club has ever had, in Steven Gerrard. Jordan has grown as a person and as a player since arriving at Liverpool and is ready to take up this challenge. He will be his own person, with his own style of leadership and his own ideas and methods." 41

JAMES MILNER

DATE OF BIRTH:
4 January 1986

BIRTHPLACE:
Horsforth

PREVIOUS CLUBS:
Leeds United, Newcastle United, Aston Villa, Manchester City

SIGNED:
July 2015

PLAYER

DATE OF BIRTH:
10 May 1988

BIRTHPLACE:
St Albans

PREVIOUS CLUBS:
Bournemouth, Southampton

SIGNED:
July 2014

ADAM LALLANA

42

DANIEL STURRIDGE

DATE OF BIRTH:
1 September 1989

BIRTHPLACE:
Birmingham

PREVIOUS CLUBS:
Manchester City,
Bolton Wanderers (loan), Chelsea

SIGNED:
January 2013

PROFILES

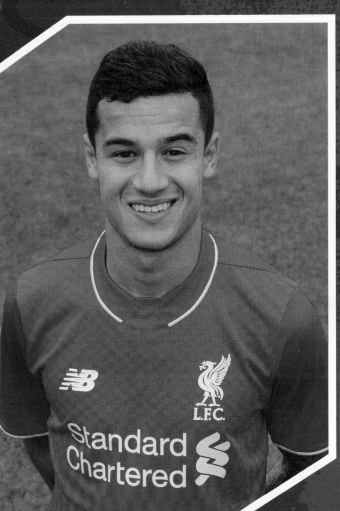

DATE OF BIRTH:
12 June 1992

BIRTHPLACE:
Rio de Janeiro, Brazil

PREVIOUS CLUBS:
Vasco da Gama,
Inter Milan, Espanyol (loan)

SIGNED:
January 2013

PHILIPPE COUTINHO

DANNY INGS

DATE OF BIRTH:
23 July 1992

BIRTHPLACE:
Winchester

PREVIOUS CLUBS:
Bournemouth, Dorchester (loan), Burnley

SIGNED:
July 2015

PLAYER PROFILES

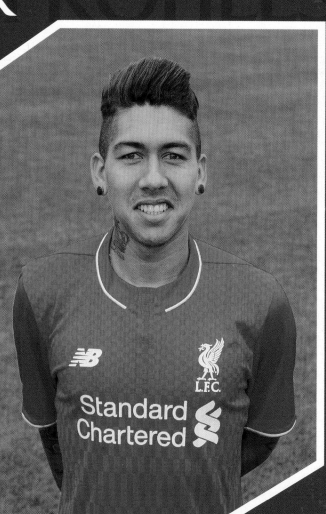

DATE OF BIRTH:
2 October 1991

BIRTHPLACE:
Maceio, Brazil

PREVIOUS CLUBS:
Figueirense, 1899 Hoffenheim

SIGNED:
July 2015

ROBERTO FIRMINO

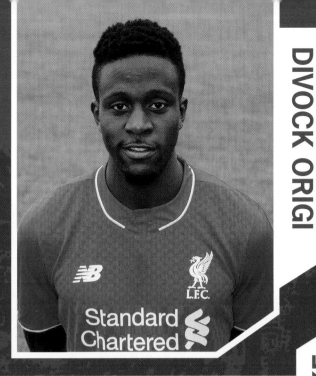

DIVOCK ORIGI

DATE OF BIRTH:
18 April 1995

BIRTHPLACE:
Ostend, Belgium

PREVIOUS CLUBS:
Genk, Lille

SIGNED:
July 2014

CHRISTIAN BENTEKE

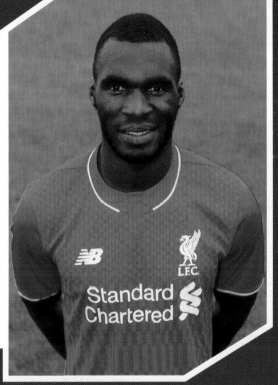

DATE OF BIRTH:
3 December 1990

BIRTHPLACE:
Kinshasa, DR Congo

PREVIOUS CLUBS:
Genk, Standard Liege, Kortrijk (loan),
Mechelen (loan), Genk, Aston Villa

SIGNED:
July 2015

PLAYER
PROFILES

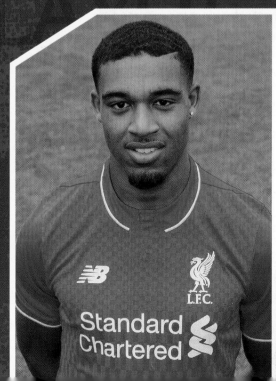

JORDON IBE

DATE OF BIRTH:
8 December 1995

BIRTHPLACE:
London

PREVIOUS CLUBS:
Wycombe Wanderers

SIGNED:
December 2011

45

LIVERPOOL FC WORDSEARCH

Find the words in the grid. Words can go horizontally, vertically and diagonally in all eight directions.

```
L F J E G D I R R U T S B
L J L V S Q Z S J F E C Q
W A M A N G A H I M L O Q
I N L N N C N R Q N O U N
T G T L U A M I A C N T O
G M I L A I G D H X G I S
R O N R N N G A S G I N R
N R L O O O A K N V M H E
N E L Q B B R M M D Q O D
E N R J N T V L K K B M N
L O K V E L G C L Y N E E
L J Z L O H K A S P X L H
A B V R P L M I L N E R K
```

Allen / Lovren / Bogdan / Lucas / Clyne / Mignolet / Coutinho / Milner / Firmino / Moreno / Flanagan / Origi / Henderson / Sakho / Ings / Skrtel / Lallana / Sturridge

SPOT THE DIFFERENCE

Study both photographs and see if you can spot the 10 differences.

THE CHANGING FACE OF ANFIELD

Anfield, one of the most iconic stadiums in world football,
is undergoing a major facelift that will soon see it transformed into an arena fit for the 21st century.

Work on the redevelopment of the Main Stand has been ongoing since January and rapid progress is being made ahead of its planned opening in August 2016.

The design of the new stand will ensure that the unrivalled atmosphere and spirit of Anfield is retained, whilst taking the full stadium capacity to 54,000.

It's set to become one of the largest all-seater single stands in Europe and will be visible from several points in the city, adding another impressive landmark to the world renowned Liverpool skyline.

21ST CENTURY ANFIELD

✓ Increase the stadium capacity to 54,000
The Main Stand will house around 20,000 seats, more than one third of the fully expanded stadium capacity

✓ Incorporate the iconic club crest into the stadium
The Club's crest and liver bird will feature prominently on the external fabric of the building

✓ Create a new home for the Hillsborough Memorial
The Hillsborough Memorial will be housed in a specially designed colonnade, accessible from the Main Stand

✓ Improve access to the stadium for our supporters and visitors
The Anfield expansion will significantly increase the current number of wheelchair viewing positions and improve disabled access and facilities at the stadium

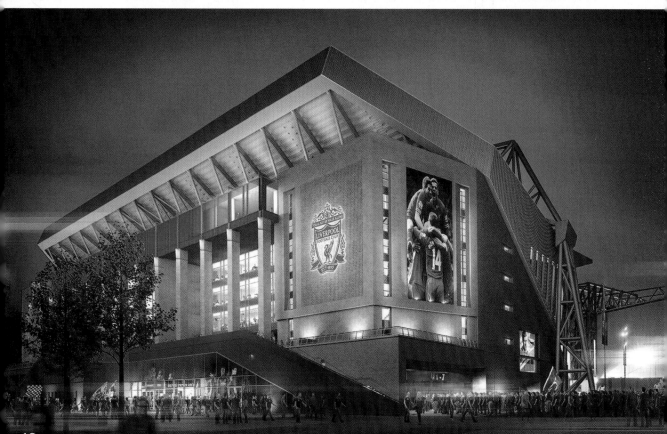

EXPANSION MILESTONES

4 Dec 2014:
LFC confirms the redevelopment of Anfield Stadium

8 Dec 2014:
First day on site for Carillion, the Club's construction partner

5 Jan 2015:
Construction work gets underway on the expansion of the Main Stand

6 Jan 2015:
The Hillsborough Memorial is placed into safe storage and a specially commissioned Temporary Memorial is erected at the entrance of the Centenary Stand where families, friends, supporters and visitors can continue to pay their respects. The eternal flame is transferred to Liverpool Cathedral, where it will reside during this temporary period

24 Feb 2015:
The Shankly Gates are placed safe into safe storage

9 Mar 2015:
The first steel is assembled at Anfield as work begins to erect the new structure behind the existing Stand

26 May 2015:
Demolition of the existing 1980s structure behind the Stand begins

5 Jun 2015:
The assembly of the Main Stand's new truss begins on site

1 Jul 2015:
The Main Stand's first 28m high tower is erected between the Kop and the existing Stand

3 July 2015:
The Main Stand's second 28m high tower is erected between the Anfield Road and the existing Stand

9 July 2015:
The first sections of the two largest cranes in the UK start to arrive on site at Anfield ahead of lifting a 650tonne roof truss above the Main Stand

24 July 2015:
Historic milestone at Anfield as the Main Stand's 650 tonne steel truss is lifted into place above the Stadium

Supporters are able to keep track of Anfield's redevelopment via regular time-lapse updates on the club's official website www.liverpoolfc.com

AWARDS NIGHT

PHILIPPE COUTINHO
TOOK CENTRE STAGE

when Liverpool Football Club staged its second Players' Awards Dinner in May 2015.

The Brazilian was the deserving winner of four individual accolades as his fine form during the 2014/15 season was officially recognised.

The attacking midfielder was voted the Reds' Player of the Year by supporters following an online vote and was also selected as the stand-out first-team performer by his colleagues at Melwood.

In addition, he also collected the 'Goal of the Season' award, for his stunning strike at Southampton, and 'Performance of the Year', for his display in the 2-1 home victory over Manchester City in March.

Elsewhere, Raheem Sterling retained the Young Player of the Year award he won last year, while

Portuguese starlet Joao Carlos Texiera scooped the Academy prize.

In recognition of everything he has done for the club during his 17 seasons in the first team, departing captain Steven G was honoured with the Outstanding Achievement Award and, 50 years on from leading Liverpool to a first FA Cup success, Kop legends Ron Yeats and Ian St John were the proud recipients of the Lifetime Achievement Award.

FULL LIST OF AWARD WINNERS

PLAYER OF THE YEAR
Philippe Coutinho

PLAYERS' PLAYER OF THE YEAR
Philippe Coutinho

GOAL OF THE YEAR
Philippe Coutinho v Southhampton (February 22)

PERFORMANCE OF THE YEAR
Philippe Coutinho v Manchester City (March 1)

YOUNG PLAYER OF THE YEAR
Raheem Sterling

OUTSTANDING ACHIEVEMENT AWARD
Steven Gerrard

ACADAMY PLAYERS' PLAYER OF THE YEAR
Joao Carlos Teixeira

LADIES PLAYERS' PLAYER OF THE YEAR
Fara Williams

LIFETIME ACHIEVEMENT AWARD
Ron Yeats and Ian St John

SUPPORTERS' CLUB OF THE YEAR
OLSC London

BILL SHANKLY COMMUNITY AWARD
Chris Anders

LFC STAFF RECOGNITION AWARD
Ian Wallace

FARA WILLIAMS: IN PROFILE

Fara Williams is one of the most famous footballers in the women's game and an influential figure at the heart of midfield for the Liverpool Ladies.

She is the most capped England player of all-time, having represented her country 146 times, and was part of the team that reached the semi-final of the World Cup in 2015.

Domestically, Williams is also highly decorated. Having previously played for Chelsea and Charlton, she joined the Reds from neighbours Everton ahead of the 2013 Super League season and played a pivotal role in the back-to-back title triumphs that followed.

DATE OF BIRTH: January 25, 1984

PLACE OF BIRTH: London

POSITION: Midfield

FIRST TEAM PLAYED FOR? Fulham

WHEN DID YOU JOIN LIVERPOOL? 2013

WHO WAS YOUR IDOL GROWING UP? Gianfranco Zola

FAVOURITE SPORT OTHER THAN FOOTBALL? Boxing

FAVOURITE SUBJECT AT SCHOOL? Maths

IF YOU WERE NOT A FOOTBALLER, WHAT JOB WOULD YOU LIKE TO DO?
A coach

FAVOURITE FOOD?
Italian

WHAT PERSON WOULD YOU MOST LIKE TO MEET?
Zinedine Zidane

WHICH LIVERPOOL PLAYER, PAST OR PRESENT, DO YOU ADMIRE?
Steven Gerrard

DESCRIBE LIVERPOOL IN ONE WORD...
Together

51

YOUNG GUNS

Life at the Liverpool Academy continues to go from strength to strength. Under the expert tutelage of coaches Michael Beale and Neil Critchley, more and more youngsters are knocking on the door of the Reds' first team. LFCTV commentator Steve Hunter has been following the fortunes of the Liverpool starlets for several years and he's picked out six of the best from the current crop...

A commanding presence between the sticks, Fulton hails from Burnley but has represented Scotland at international level. He's been with Liverpool since under-10 level and has made great progress. A superb shot stopper, he has already played in the UEFA Youth League and trained at Melwood alongside Simon Mignolet during the 2014/15 season. He has everything in his locker to be a top goalkeeper.

RYAN FULTON

RYAN KENT

Oldham-born Ryan Kent is an explosive talent. A natural winger who can also play as a number ten, he is exciting to watch when in full flow and a nightmare for the opposing defence. A level headed lad, Kent has been at the Academy since the age of seven and is capable of scoring some fantastic goals, as he proved when netting a double against Everton in the under-21s derby at Goodison Park last season.

This former MK Dons starlet is another player of immense potential. A pacy winger who can operate anywhere across the front line, he joined the club in 2011 and after starting out in the under-18s team has since made the step up to the under-21s. The time he spent on loan will have done him the world of good and in the words of Kop legend John Aldridge, one of my co-commentators on LFCTV, 'this lad can be anything he wants to be.'

SHEYI OJO

JORDAN ROSSITER

This tenacious young Scouser enjoyed a memorable first team debut last season and is more than capable of adding to that. Comparisons with fellow midfielder Steven Gerrard are unfair but it's easy to see why they are made. Both are local lads who play in the same position and, like Gerrard, Rossiter also possesses great leadership skills, having captained Liverpool's UEFA Youth League team. He may have already tasted life in the first team but his feet have remained firmly on the ground and he's certainly one to keep an eye on.

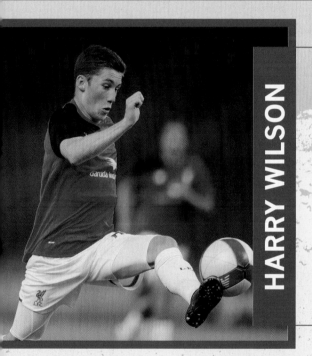

HARRY WILSON

Although he's yet to make his senior bow for the Reds there's a definite buzz about the potential of young Wilson and already he's won a full cap for Wales. A very talented dribbler who can cause havoc to any defence, he is also deadly with free-kicks and scored the Academy's goal of 2014-15 with the last minute winner for the under-21s against Everton. He's made great progress so far and there's much more to come from him.

Jordan Williams is a Welsh youth international who can play centre-back, right-back or as a holding midfielder. At under-21 level he has shown great maturity and an ability to dominate games. For someone so young he has such a reassuring presence about him and, by scoring a penalty in front of the Kop when making his first team debut last season, has already proved that the step up to senior level would not faze him.

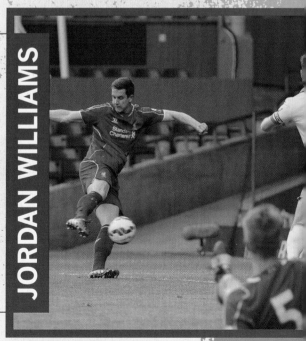

JORDAN WILLIAMS

SUMMER TOUR 2015

Liverpool returned to Australia as part of their 2015 summer tour and, yet again, it was a trip to remember.

Games in Adelaide and Brisbane were sandwiched in between visits to Bangkok in Thailand and Kuala Lumpur in Malaysia.

Two years after the Reds last toured this part of the world the supporters again turned out in force to savour what was a rare opportunity to see their heroes in the flesh and their burning passion for the club was clearly evident in each of the destinations. On the pitch it was also a profitable exercise for Brendan Rodgers and his team as they tuned up for the new season with three wins and a draw.

TOUR SQUAD

Simon Mignolet, Adam Bogdan, Alberto Moreno, Joe Gomez, Nathaniel Clyne, Mamadou Sakho, Martin Skrtel, Dejan Lovren, Andre Wisdom, Lucas, Joe Allen, James Milner, Jordan Henderson, Jordon Ibe, Lazar Markovic, Divock Origi, Danny Ings, Ricky Lambert, Ryan Fulton, Joe Maguire, Dan Cleary, Jordan Rossiter, Pedro Chirivella, Ryan Kent, Sheyi Ojo, Harry Wilson, Joao Carlos Teixeira

RESULTS
Thai All-Stars 4-0
Brisbane Roar 2-1
Adelaide United 2-0
Malaysia XI 1-1

2014-2015
SEASON IN STATS

The following players made their Liverpool first team debuts during 2014/15...

Name	PL	FA	LC	CL	EL	Total
Jordan Henderson	37	7	4	5	1	54
Simon Mignolet	36	7	3	6	2	54
Philippe Coutinho	35	7	4	5	1	52
Raheem Sterling	35	5	4	6	2	52
Martin Skrtel	33	5	3	5	2	48
Steven Gerrard	29	3	3	6	0	41
Adam Lallana	27	4	4	4	2	41
Alberto Moreno	28	4	2	5	2	41
Emre Can	27	6	3	2	2	40
Dejan Lovren	26	4	2	4	2	38
Rickie Lambert	25	4	3	3	1	36
Lazar Markovic	19	6	5	4	0	34
Lucas Leiva	20	3	5	4	0	32
Joe Allen	21	5	0	4	2	32
Glen Johnson	19	4	2	3	0	28
Mario Balotelli	16	4	3	3	2	28
Mamadou Sakho	16	4	4	1	1	27
Kolo Toure	12	3	3	2	1	21
Javier Manquillo	10	2	2	4	1	19
Daniel Sturridge	12	4	0	0	2	18
Fabio Borini	12	2	2	2	0	18
Jordon Ibe	12	0	0	0	2	14
Jose Enrique	4	2	1	2	0	9
Brad Jones	3	0	2	0	0	5
Jerome Sinclair	2	0	0	0	0	2
Jordan Rossiter	0	0	1	0	0	1
Suso	0	0	1	0	0	1
Jordan Williams	0	0	1	0	0	1

RICKIE LAMBERT
17.08.2014
v Southampton

DEJAN LOVREN
17.08.2014
v Southampton

JAVIER MANQUILLO
17.08.2014
v Southampton

ALBERTO MORENO
25.08.2014
v Manchester City

EMRE CAN
25.08.2014
v Manchester City

LAZAR MARKOVIC
25.08.2014
v Manchester City

MARIO BALOTELLI
31.08.2014
v Tottenham

ADAM LALLANA
13.09.2014
v Aston Villa

JORDAN ROSSITER
23.09.2014
v Middlesbrough

JORDAN WILLIAMS
23.09.2014
v Middlesbrough

Name	PL	LC	FA	CL	EL	Total
Steven Gerrard	9	0	2	2	0	13
Raheem Sterling	7	3	1	0	0	11
Philippe Coutinho	5	0	3	0	0	8
Jordan Henderson	6	0	0	1	0	7
Adam Lallana	5	0	1	0	0	6
Daniel Sturridge	4	0	1	0	0	5
Own goals	4	0	0	0	0	4
Mario Balotelli	1	1	0	1	0	4
Lazar Markovic	2	1	0	0	1	3
Rickie Lambert	2	0	0	1	0	3
Alberto Moreno	2	0	0	0	0	2
Emre Can	1	0	0	0	0	1
Dejan Lovren	0	1	0	0	0	1
Jordan Rossiter	0	1	0	0	0	1
Glen Johnson	1	0	0	0	0	1
Martin Skrtel	1	0	0	0	0	1
Fabio Borini	1	0	0	0	0	1
Suso	0	1	0	0	0	1
Joe Allen	1	0	0	0	0	1

Liverpool's highest league position during 2014/15 was 5th

Liverpool's lowest league position during 2014/15 was 12th

Liverpool's final Premier League finishing position was 6th

Liverpool's biggest win was 3-0 away to Tottenham Hotspur & 4-1 at home to Swansea

Liverpool's highest-scoring fixture was the 1-6 defeat away to Stoke City

Liverpool's heaviest defeat was 1-6 away to Stoke City

Liverpool's average home attendance was 44,238

Liverpool registered a total of 74 goals during 2014/15, split as follows...

Premier League - **52**
FA Cup - **8**
League Cup - **8**
Champions League - **5**
Europa League – **1**
In total, Liverpool played 58 competitive games in 2014/15 – winning **26**, drawing **14** and losing **18**

In Player	Club	Date
Rickie Lambert	Southampton	2 June 2014
Adam Lallana	Southampton	1 July 2014
Emre Can	Leverkusen	3 July 2014
Lazar Markovic	Benfica	15 July 2014
Dejan Lovren	Southampton	27 July 2014
Divick Origi	Lille	29 July 2014
Javier Manquillo	Atletico Madrid	6 August 2014
Alberto Moreno	Sevilla	16 August 2014
Mario Balotelli	AC Milan	25 August 2014
Out Player	**Club**	**Date**
Luis Suarez	Barcelona	16 July 2014
Conor Coady	Huddersfield Town	6 August 2014
Pepe Reina	Bayern Munich	8 August 2014
Martin Kelly	Crystal Palace	14 August 2014
Kristoffer Peterson	Utrecht	27 August 2014
Jack Robinson	QPR	28 August 2014
Daniel Agger	Brøndby	30 August 2014
Oussama Assaidi	Al Ahli	12 January 2015
Suso	AC Milan	17 January 2015

"AND FOR LIVERPOOOOOOOL!"

Meet Peter McDowall, the man behind the match day mic at Anfield.

Peter, can you describe your match day role at Anfield? My role is essentially to announce the team, the most important information given over the tannoy on any match day! Times have changed and most people already know, because of social media and websites, by the time they get inside the ground but there's still a bit of magic about calling out the players that have been entrusted with going after the three points. I also do any announcements that are needed on the day, and maybe some half time presentations - but essentially it's about telling people who will be out on the pitch.

You've become known for the unique style in which you read out the Liverpool team – was this a conscious decision on your part or did it just evolve?

It actually came from Phil too, I remember asking him about his style and how he announced players' names. He always gave Steven Gerrard and Jamie Carragher big shouts because they were local players, Fernando Torres too. But he had this catchphrase, a simple one - but he would announce the away team, then leave a big gap and say "....And for Liverpoooool" then a big cheer would go up. I didn't plan to continue it, it didn't seem right because it was his thing, but his brother was keen for me to so I did. Mine is slightly more dramatic, as was my announcement around Luis Suarez, but he was magical - and away fans dreaded seeing him so it was all part of the fun.

Have you ever got a player's name wrong or what has been the most difficult to announce? There are lots that are very difficult to announce, but my technique is to say those names very quickly and hope nobody notices! I remember having problems announcing Sotirios Kyrgiakos, it was little wonder his teammates just called him 'Sotto'.

You've interviewed quite a few famous people on the pitch at half-time, what has been the most memorable and why?
I've been so lucky, I've introduced so many of the new signings, said emotional farewells to Jamie Carragher and more recently Steven Gerrard. I can also remember bringing out most of Bill Shankly's iconic signings on his birthday while his family watched and bag pipers played Amazing Grace, his favourite hymn. It was so emotional and I had the biggest lump in my throat. I have to say Pele was the biggest thrill, he is arguably the best footballer that's ever lived and he was my grandad's hero so I was thrilled to get the chance to speak to him.

Is there anyone that you're still in awe of when you meet them? I'm lucky that so many of the people I was in awe of as a young football fan I have been able to meet and in many cases become friends with, and they are just like you and I, even if it takes a while to get used to being around them. Kenny Dalglish still has an aura about him though, he lights up any room he walks into.

What do you most enjoy about your role? I enjoy everything about it really, I'm incredibly lucky to be able to see the matches and, even more, to have a job working there. The big games; Everton, Manchester United and the European nights all create a special atmosphere and announcing the team names to a massive roar is a big rush, so if I had to pick something I would say that.

We know what you do of a match-day, can you tell us a bit more about what else you do throughout the week? I work for Liverpool full time, as a presenter on LFCTV so a lot of that will be either in our city centre offices presenting shows on the channel, or based at the training ground producing news programmes or interviewing the players. We are lucky enough to follow the team home and away so get to travel with them in this country and abroad, including the pre-season tours during the summer.

What is more nerve-wracking – reading out the Liverpool team or presenting live TV? That's a tough one. I would say reading the team out!

What advice would you give to anyone hoping to following in your footsteps? I always wanted to be a radio presenter when I was younger, and I did everything I could to put myself in a position where I could achieve that. I went into local weekly newspapers to shadow reporters, did hospital radio for years and then studied journalism at university. But my biggest thing was listening to as much radio as I could, listening to how presenters spoke and how they commentated on football matches, how they painted the pictures with their words. Anyone who wants to get into the job has to be a student of it, watch as many presenters as you can, adopt your own style but learn from the good and bad. The thing people say to me most often is 'you're so lucky' and I am so thankful for the job I do, but you only get lucky with hard work · and you don't stay lucky for long without it. The harder you work the luckier you get.

COMPETITION

Answer the following question correctly and you could win a Liverpool FC shirt signed by a first team player.

In what year was Liverpool Football Club formed?

a. 1902   b. 1892   c. 1899

Entry is by email only. Only one entry per contestant. Please enter LFC SHIRT followed by either A, B or C in the subject line of an email. In the body of the email, please include your full name, address, postcode, email address and phone number and send to:

frontdesk@grangecommunications.co.uk by Friday 24 March 2016.

TERMS AND CONDITIONS

1) The closing date for this competition is Friday the 25th March 2016 at midnight. Entries received after that time will not be counted.
2) Information on how to enter and on the prizes form part of these conditions.
3) Entry is open to those residing in the UK only. If entrants are under 18, consent from a parent or guardian must be obtained and the parent or guardian must agree to these terms and conditions.
4) This competition is not open to employees or their relatives of Liverpool FC. Any such entries will be invalid.
5) The start date for entries is 31st October 2015 at 4pm.
6) Entries must be strictly in accordance with these terms and conditions. Any entry not in strict accordance with these terms and conditions will be deemed to be invalid and no prizes will be awarded in respect of such entry. By entering, all entrants will be deemed to accept these rules.
7) One (1) lucky winner will win a 2015/2016 season signed football shirt.
8) The prize is non-transferable and no cash alternative will be offered. Entry is by email only. Only one entry per contestant. Please enter LFC SHIRT followed by either A, B or C in the subject line of an email. In the body of the email, please include your full name, address, postcode, email address and phone number and send to: frontdesk@grangecommunications.co.uk by Friday 24 March 2016.
9) The winner will be picked at random. The winner will be contacted within 72 hours of the closing date. Details of the winners can be requested after this time from the address below.
10) Entries must not be sent in through agents or third parties. No responsibility can be accepted for lost, delayed, incomplete, or for electronic entries or winning notifications that are not received or delivered. Any such entries will be deemed void.
11) The winners shall have 72 hours to claim their prize once initial contact has been made by the Promoter. Failure to respond may result in forfeiture of the prize.
12) On entering the competition you are allowing Liverpool Football Club and its trusted partners to contact you with information about products and services they believe might be of interest to you. If you do not wish to receive any marketing information from the Club, you can opt out by emailing LFC STOP to frontdesk@grangecommunications.co.uk before midnight on Friday 24th March 2016
13) The Promoter reserves the right to withdraw or amend the promotion as necessary due to circumstances outside its reasonable control. The Promoter's decision on all matters is final and no correspondence will be entered into.
14) The Promoter (or any third party nominated by the Promoter) may use the winner's name and image and their comments relating to the prize for future promotional, marketing and publicity purposes in any media worldwide without notice or without any fee being paid.
15) Liverpool Football Club's decision is final, no correspondence will be entered in to. Except in respect of death or personal injury resulting from any negligence of the Club, neither The Liverpool Football Club nor any of its officers, employees or agents shall be responsible for (whether in tort, contract or otherwise):
   (i)   any loss, damage or injury to you and/or any guest or to any property belonging to you or any guest in connection with this competition and/or the prize, resulting from any cause whatsoever;
   (ii) for any loss of profit, loss of use, loss of opportunity or any indirect, economic or consequential losses whatsoever;
16) This competition shall be governed by English law.
17) Promoter: Grange Communications, 22 Great King Street, Edinburgh EH3 6QH

Last year's winner- Lewis Brown

QUIZ AND PUZZLE ANSWERS

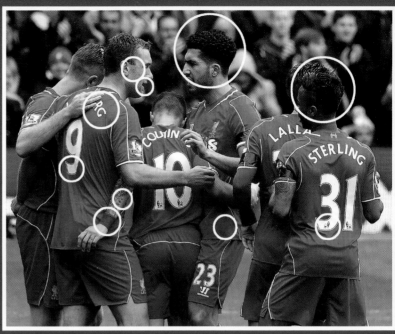

p.46: WORDSEARCH

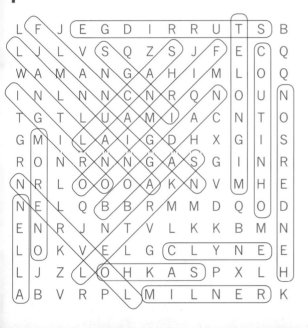

p. 26 – 27: THE BIG KOP QUIZ

1. Hoffenheim
2. Villa Park
3. Philippe Coutinho
4. Huddersfield Town
5. Bangkok
6. Borussia Monchengladbach
7. Tiago Ilori
8. Jordan Rossiter
9. Total Netword Solutions
10. Belgium
11. White
12. Daniel Sturridge
13. Phil Neal
14. Luis Suarez
15. Four
16. Fara Williams
17. True
18. False
19. False
20. True
21. Nick Barmby
22. Kevin Keegan
23. Yossi Benayoun
24. 1964
25. 1977
26. 1988
27. 2007
28. Aston Villa
29. 1976
30. Dietmar Hamann

WHERE'S MIGHTY RED?
SOMEWHERE HIDDEN IN THE CROWD IS,
CAN YOU FIND HIM?